the Art of Creating

Ideas for Children's Rooms and Parties

WHITE STAR PUBLISHERS

Contents

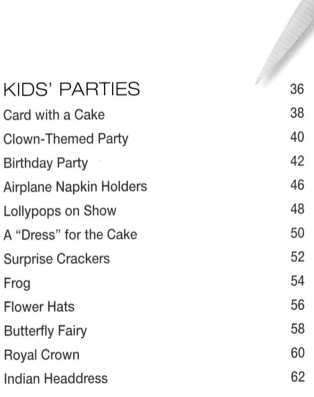

The Tools

Children, as we all know, bring cheerfulness, joy, color and a good deal of confusion into a house. If you want to decorate the rooms of the smallest members of the family in an original and creative way, by creating a joyful, welcoming and reassuring environment inspired by the children's favorite characters, animals and fantastical creatures, just follow the detailed instructions contained in the following pages. In these pages, you will also find a wide range of wonderful ideas for making child parties special and unforgettable.

- Alphabet stamps
- Black permanent marker
- Brushes for stenciling (stencil and round)
- Cardboard 1x3 in. (4x8 cm)
- Circle craft punch (1 in. [2.5 cm], 1 1/8 in. [2.8 cm], 1 1/4 in. [3 cm] in diameter)
- Clocks stamp
- Clothespins
- Compass

- Compass with adaptor
- Compass with extension bar
- Cotton swabs
- Cutting mat
- Decorative-edge scissors
- Eraser
- Flat-tipped paintbrush
- Glasses
- Hand-held hole punch (1/8 in. [3 mm] in diameter)
- Hatpin

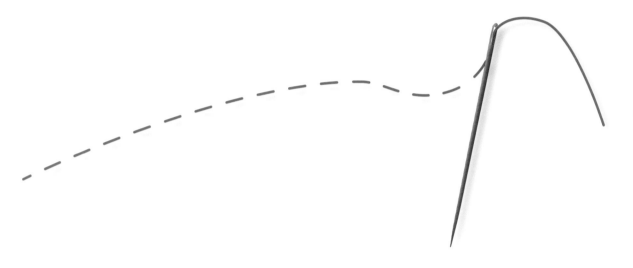

- Hole punch (1/8 in. [3 mm],
  5/32 in. [4 mm] in diameter)
- Manual riveter
- Medium hole punch
- Needle
- Nippers
- Paper clamps
- Pencil
- Pencil sharpener
- Precision knife
- Punch
- Riveting kit (hammer and punch)

- Rotary cutter
- Round-tipped paintbrush
- Ruler
- Scallop-edge scissors
- Scissors
- Sponge
- Stapler
- Tulip craft punch
- Twine (20 in., 50 cm)
- Utility knife
- Wavy-edge scissors

Children's Rooms

In the Savanna

Materials

▶ Contact paper: wood, leather, cork, wicker, green velvet, pink checkered fabric and patterned in tones of blue
▶ Black embroidery thread
▶ Black raffia
▶ "Eye" stickers
▶ Reusable adhesive squares
▶ Masking tape

Diff./Time

Easy

⧗ ⧗ ⧗
1 hour

Transform a bedroom or a bathroom into an African savanna with these lovable wild animal stickers.

1 Draw the Motifs

Cut out templates from photocopies of the drawings on the right. Place them on the back of the contact paper and trace with a pencil: place them face down or face up depending on the composition desired (you can trace some branches and flowers facing right and others facing left). Cut out the motifs with scissors.

3 Create the Details

Attach the "eye" stickers. Cut pieces of black embroidery thread for the lashes and insert them behind the eyes. Insert pieces of raffia starting from the head and down the neck to create the mane.

IDEA. Complete the composition by attaching paper or plastic insects with pieces of reusable adhesive squares.

Enlarge the diagrams to the desired size.

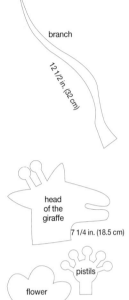

branch

12 1/2 in. (32 cm)

head of the giraffe

7 1/4 in. (18.5 cm)

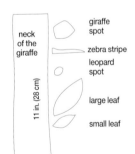

pistils

flower

neck of the giraffe

11 in. (28 cm)

giraffe spot

zebra stripe

leopard spot

large leaf

small leaf

2 Compose the Scene

Attach all the components to the surface to decorate to see the effect achieved. Start with the branches: attach them temporarily with pieces of masking tape.

Attach the Motifs

Remove the protective backing from the components one by one and attach them. Start with the background components: first attach the branches, next the neck and the head of the giraffe, and then the spots, leaves, pistils and flowers. To camouflage the seams between the branches, cover them with flowers and leaves.

VARIATIONS

To make the zebra, make the neck shorter and adhere the stripes; for the mane, use black embroidery thread.

To make the leopard, make the neck even shorter; cut out and adhere the spots; for the whiskers, make a nick in the muzzle and insert pieces of black embroidery thread.

Wall Containers

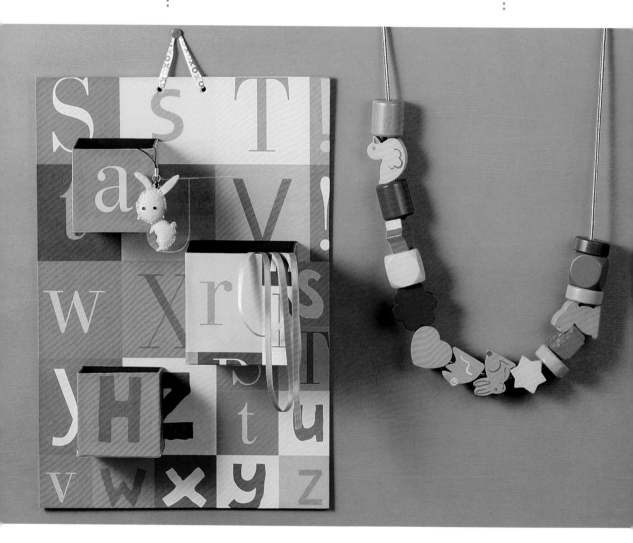

Decorate a wall of the children's room with this panel of knickknack containers covered in multi-colored letters.

1 Assemble the Boxes

Cut ten 3 in. (7.5 cm) squares of finn-board (for the two small boxes) and five 4 in. (10 cm) squares (for the large box). Dampen the Kraft gummed paper tape with a sponge and use it to assemble the boxes. Cut away excess tape with scissors.

2 Paint the Boxes

Using acrylic paint, color the inside of each box. Allow to dry and, if necessary, apply a second coat of paint.

3 Cover the Panel

Apply a coat of Elmer's glue to the surface of the foam board rectangle and cover with the sheet of paper decorated with letters. Fold the paper over the edges and glue down with a small amount of Elmer's glue.

4 Cover the Boxes

Cut three 3x3 1/4 in. (7.5x8.5 cm) rectangles and two 3 in. (7.5 cm) squares for each small box, and three 4 1/8x4 1/2 in. (10.5x11.5 cm) rectangles and two 4 in. (10 cm) squares for the large box. Brush glue onto the boxes and adhere the paper onto the various faces, folding the excess onto adjacent faces (to hide the excess, start with the rectangles and finish with the squares).

5 Make the Holes

Glue each box to the panel with Elmer's glue. Use an appropriate hole punch to make two holes 1 3/4 in. (4.5 cm) apart, 1/2 in. (1 cm) from the top edge and centered along the width. Thread the ribbon through the holes from front to back of the panel and tie.

IDEA. You can cover the panel and boxes with pieces of paper of the same color and glue colored carton letters on top.

Glue On the Paper Without Making a Mess

To avoid getting glue onto the working surface, line it with a piece of white paper. Set the object to be coated onto a sheet of paper and brush on an even coat of Elmer's glue. Change the paper, every time it gets dirty with glue to avoid getting it onto the surface of the next object. Don't use newspapers because the glue may make the ink run. Save used computer or notebook paper to use for your collage projects.

A Miniature Room

Tools

- Pencil
- Ruler
- Utility knife
- Cutting mat
- Scissors
- Scallop-edge scissors
- Tulip craft punch
- Needle
- Flat-tipped paintbrush

Materials

- 8x8 in. (20x20 cm) card stock cookie box base, 2 in. (5 cm) tall
- Foam board, 1/8 in. (3 mm) and 3/16 (5 mm) thick
- Card stock 1/16 in. (1 mm) thick
- Floral, blue checkered, green patterned and fuchsia patterned scrapbooking paper
- A magazine cut-out of the sky
- Tracing paper
- Embossed paper (or cupcake liners)
- Pink embroidery thread
- Blue wood bead
- 3D letter stickers
- Elmer's glue
- Universal fast-drying adhesive
- Adhesive tape
- Double-sided adhesive foam pads

Diff./Time

Difficult

2 hours

With a little bit of work you can create this brightly-colored three-dimensional artwork that's great for a little girl's room.

1 Line the Interior

Cut a 6x12 1/4 in. (15x31 cm) rectangle of the floral scrapbooking paper (top of the wall) and one 2 1/4x12 1/4 in. (6x31 cm) from the blue checkered scrapbooking paper (bottom of the wall). Coat the inside of the box with these strips using Elmer's glue. Cut two 8x2 1/2 in. (20x6 cm) strips of green scrapbooking paper (ceiling and floor) and glue to the inside of the box. Fold excess paper over the edges of the box.

2 Make the Window

Trace the diagram in the lower left onto card stock. Cut along the lines. Coat with glue and adhere to the center of a 4 1/8x3 in. (10.5x7.5 cm) rectangle of blue checkered scrapbooking paper. Make 45° cute in the protruding corners. Incise the paper in the window opening to form flaps. Spread glue onto the flaps and fold them over the edges. Glue the 2 1/4x3 1/2 in. (6x9 cm) rectangle with the image of the sky behind the window. Glue the window 2 3/4 in. (7 cm) from the floor and 1 1/4 in. (3 cm) from the right-hand wall.

3 Make the Vignettes

Cut four 5/8 in. (1.6 cm) wide strips of card stock: one 8 in. (20 cm), one 3 in. (8 cm) and two 1 3/4 in. (4.5 cm) long. From the fuchsia paper, cut two 1 1/4 in. (3 cm), one 8 in. (20 cm) and one 3 in. (8 cm) wide strips; and punch out evenly spaced tulips. Cut two more 1 1/4x1 3/4 in. (3x4.5 cm) fuchsia strips. Cover each card stock strip with a fuchsia strip of the same length, folding excess paper over the edges.

4 Make the Ceiling Lamp

Cut out three identical flowers from the floral scrapbooking paper. Glue them together giving them the shape of a conical hat. Cut out four identical flowers and glue each pair back to back to form two flowers. Make a cut in each flower along the radius and slide them together. Cut a length of the pink thread, thread through a needle and tie a double knot at the end. Pass the thread through the lampshade, and the bead, glue to the flowers and pass through the ceiling. Secure the thread with two pieces of adhesive tape.

Enlarge the diagram by 240%.

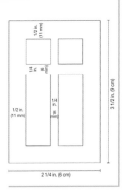

5 Assemble

Glue the 8 in. (20 cm) vignette over the junction of the two scrapbooking papers. Glue two 1 3/4 in. (4.5 cm) strips to the sidewalls. Glue two 1 1/4x3 1/2 in. (3x9 cm) rectangles cut from the embossed paper to the back of the 3 in. (8 cm) vignette. Attach the vignette with the "curtains" to the front of the window using two adhesive foam pads. Make the frame.

Adjust the Frame to Fit the Display

Cut a 10 1/2 in. (27 cm) square from the 1/8 in. (3 mm) thick foam board. From the center, cut out a 7 1/4 in. (18.5 cm) square. Cut four 3x10 1/2 in. (8x27 cm) strips of green scrapbooking paper and cut the ends at 45°. Glue the strips to the foam board folding the excess over the edges. Center the display over the frame and trace the edges. Cut four strips of 3/16 in. (5 mm) thick foam board: two 8 1/2x3/4 in. (21.5x2 cm) and two 8 1/8x3/4 in. (20.5x2 cm). Coat the edges of the strips with glue and adhere outside the trace lines pressing down hard. Wrap the foam board sides with adhesive tape and insert the display. Compose words with the letter stickers.

One Plus One...

Tools	Materials	Diff./Time
▶ Pencil ▶ Ruler ▶ Utility knife ▶ Cutting mat ▶ Scissors	▶ Three small 3 in. (8 cm) square wood frames ▶ Thre color headshots ▶ Three 11 3/4 in. (30 cm) squares of patterned scrapbooking paper ▶ 2x4 in. (5x10 cm) foam board, 3/16 in. (5 mm) thick ▶ Three baby-themed stickers ▶ Universal fast-drying adhesive	 **Easy** **45 min.**

These three sweet floral frames form a mathematical equation full of meaning: a perfect addition to the nursery.

1 Cut the Paper

Draw and cut out three 4 3/4 in. (12 cm) squares of scrapbooking paper. Apply the fast-drying adhesive to one of the frames and glue it to the back of a paper square, centering well. Make incisions in the opening of the frame using a precision knife.

Make Incisions in the Paper

To avoid tearing the paper when you cut open the central openings, make a cut from one corner to the center, then start a new cut from the opposite corner and link it with the first.

2 Fold the Edges (1)

Fold over and glue down the paper on two opposite sides of the frame. Smooth well with your fingers. Using scissors, cut the corners of the rectangles.

IDEA. Substitute the stickers with fun buttons, which you can purchase at your local crafts store.

3 Fold the Edges (2)

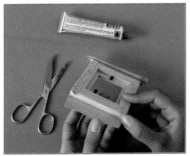

Fold over and glue down the paper along the other two sides. Using scissors, remove excess paper. Smooth well with your fingers.

4 Assemble

On the foam board, draw and cut out the "+" sign and the "=" sign (lines should be 1/2 in. [1 cm] thick). Using fast-drying adhesive, link pairs of frames with each sign. Adhere a sticker to each frame.

TRICK. You can crop the photographs to the 2x2 in. (5x5 cm) format on the computer.

Acrobats

Tools

- Pencil
- Pencil sharpener
- Ruler
- Utility knife
- Cutting mat
- Scissors
- Nippers
- Flat-tipped brush
- Round-tipped brush

Materials

- Cardboard egg carton
- Assorted acrylic paints
- Black permanent marker
- 8 in. (20 cm), round cross-section, wood rod with a diameter of 1/4 in. (5 mm)
- Five wood spheres with a diameter of 3/4 in. (2 cm)
- Wood bead with a diameter of 1 3/4 in. (4.5 cm)
- Three wood toothpicks
- Three paper mache balls
- 60 in. (150 cm) of silver aluminum wire (semi-rigid)
- Four pink rivets
- Universal fast-drying adhesive
- Elmer's glue

Diff./Time

Medium

2 hours

Delight the little ones by hanging up this baby mobile with acrobats that move at the slightest breeze over the crib.

16

1 Cut Out the Acrobats

Cut four cells from the egg carton with a utility knife. Using scissors, shape the edges to make arms, legs, hands and feet. Cut out three small circles as well.

2 Paint

Paint the pants and the shirts of every acrobat with the acrylic paint that you prefer (both outside and inside the cells). Take the three paper mache balls and paint as desired.

IDEA. The baby mobile has three arms and can also be hung against a wall. If you want to make a ceiling mobile, add another three arms with four identical acrobats (to make sure it's balanced).

IDEA. Paint any details you wish on the acrobat's clothes (belts, pockets, buttons, collars) with a fine-tipped paintbrush, and black and white acrylic paints.

3 Assemble the Acrobats

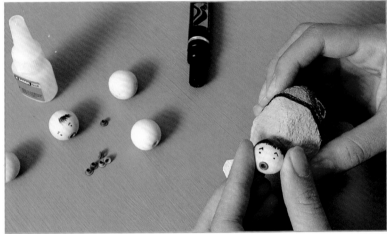

Using fast-drying adhesive, glue the rivets inside one of the openings in each wood bead with a diameter of 3/4 in. (2 cm). Using the black marker, draw the eyes, eyebrows and hair. Glue the heads to the cells with the fast-drying adhesive.

Create various poses for the acrobats

Vary the position of the head with respect to the body depending on the pose of the characters. Three acrobats have their heads glued facing the outside, while the head of the fourth faces in. Two of the acrobats are glued so they face each other.

4 Secure the String

Cut 16 in. (40 cm) of aluminum wire with the nippers. Push one end of the wire through the center of an acrobat and curl it on itself. Using fast-drying adhesive, glue one of the small cardboard circles over the loop. Do the same with the other characters.

5 Assemble the Mobile

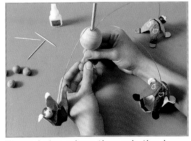

Thread the wires through the large wood bead, pulling about 2 1/4 in. (6 cm) of their length through. Drip a few dots of fast-drying adhesive into the bead. Insert the rod and three toothpicks to block everything in place. Attach a ball of paper mache to the end of each wire using fast-drying adhesive.

6 Finish the Mobile

Using the pencil sharpener, sharpen the tip of the rod. Cut 2 1/4 in. (6 cm) piece of metal wire and bend it in two. Thread the ends of the wire through the remaining bead and fold back the last 1/8 in. (3 mm). Put a little bit of Elmer's glue onto the tip of the rod and insert into the bead.

The Animal Mobile

Tools

- Pencil
- Ruler
- Utility knife
- Cutting mat
- Scissors
- Hole punch (1/8 in. [3 mm] in diameter)
- Needle

Materials

- A4 card stock sheets: purple, fuchsia, orange, pink, green, light blue, lilac and white
- Satin ribbons about 7 in. (18 cm) long: one green, one red, two orange, one light blue and one fuchsia
- Twelve small white paper fasteners
- Two wood beads (one big and one small)
- 11 3/4 in. (30 cm) of white twine
- Universal fast-drying adhesive
- Elmer's glue

Diff./Time

Medium

1 hour

Decorate the children's room with this mobile of horses and pigs that move with the breeze.

1 Cut Out the Mobile

Photocopy the drawing to the right onto the purple card stock. Using a utility knife, cut along all the solid lines. Place the trapezoid onto the orange card stock. Trace six times and cut out. Cut six 3 1/2x1/16 in. (8.8x0.2 cm) strips from the lilac card stock.

2 Construct the Mobile

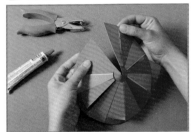

Glue the orange trapezoids between the flaps with fast-drying adhesive. Glue the thin strips to the left sides of the orange trapezoids. Punch a hole in the center of the mobile with the hand-held hole punch. Make a cone by gluing side A (in gray) under side B.

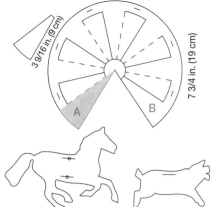

Enlarge the templates by 550% in a photocopier.

SUGGESTION. *If you don't have card stock, you can glue together two pieces of paper.*

IDEA. *Instead of the bead, you can use a small toy that your child likes.*

3 Cut Out the Animals

Photocopy the animals onto white card stock and cut them out. Cut twelve rectangles about 2x2 3/4 in. (5x7 cm) in size from colored card stock. Glue them together in pairs. Position the pig template on the rectangles and trace it. Using a utility knife, cut along the pencil marks and the slit. Cut ten 2 3/4x4 in. (7x10 cm) rectangles of colored card stock and glue them together in pairs. Trace the horse onto the rectangles and cut it out (cut the slit in just three of the horses).

Pair the Colors

Glue together different color rectangles in combinations that you like best: orange and green, fuchsia and lilac, light blue and orange, lilac and light blue, fuchsia and orange, orange and lilac etc.

4 Attach the Ribbons

Pass the ribbons through the slits in the animals and the roof. Fold the end of each ribbon against the roof, pierce it with a needle and insert paper fasteners. String the pigs onto the opposite ends of three ribbons (every other ribbon). Fold the ends of these three ribbons, pierce with the needle and insert paper fasteners. Thread a horse at the end of the other three ribbons. Fold over, pierce and insert paper fasteners.

5 Attach the Twine

Make a loop of about 2 1/4 in. (6 cm) in the twine and pass it through the hole in the roof from below. String on the small bead and make a knot at the base of the loop, below the roof. Make holes in the two remaining horses where shown on the drawing. Thread on one horse 4 in. (10 cm) and the other 8 in. (20 cm) from the roof. String on the large bead 4 in. (10 cm) from the second horse and tie with twine.

Baby Clothes Hangers

Tools

▶ Pencil
▶ Ruler
▶ Utility knife
▶ Cutting mat
▶ Scissors

Materials

▶ 11 3/4x11 3/4 in. (30x30 cm) corrugated paper, blue and pink
▶ White construction paper A4
▶ Universal fast-drying adhesive

Diff./Time

Easy

1 hour

Make original clothes hangers for your little one's layette set:
pink for the girls and blue for the boys!

1 Cut Out the Components

Carefully Trace and Cut Out

Transfer the drawing onto the back of the blue corrugated paper (with the ribbing oriented vertically). Cut along the lines (including round the heart at the center) using the utility knife and scissors. Place the cut-out on the back of the pink corrugated paper (horizontal ribbing). Trace and cut out leaving a 3/8 in. (1 cm) border all around (you will trim it once the hanger is assembled).

Transfer the drawing on the bottom of this page onto corrugated paper. Cut along the lines, including around the heart in the center.

2 Glue On the Heart

Trace a heart on scraps of pink corrugated paper (orient the ribbing horizontally). Cut it out leaving a 3/8 in. (1 cm) border all around. Apply glue along the edge of the heart (on the side of the ribbing) and glue it to the back of the blue hanger in correspondence with the opening.

IDEA. *Make hangers of different colors to easily distinguish different sizes clothes: pink/blue for "newborn," blue/green for "3 months" etc.*

3 Glue the Core

Trace the outline of the drawing on white card stock (don't trace the heart). Cut 1/4 in. (5 mm) inside the trace line. Glue the resulting shape onto the back of the blue hanger.

4 Assemble the Components

Glue the blue hanger on top of the pink. Allow to dry and trim the pink paper by running the blade along the edge of the blue paper.

Enlarge the drawing by 330% in a photocopier.

21

Socks in Order

Tools

▶ Pencil
▶ Ruler
▶ Utility knife
▶ Cutting mat
▶ Scissors
▶ Clothespins
▶ Hatpin

Materials

▶ White corrugated paper
▶ 11 3/4 in. (30 cm) square of blue patterned scrapbooking paper (horizontal stripes, vertical stripes, polka dot, checkered, with circles)
▶ Ten blue paper fasteners of different shapes and colors

▶ About 29 1/2 in. (75 cm) of whte and blue checkered ribbon, 3/8 in. (1 cm) wide
▶ Blue buttons
▶ Glue dots for small objectss
▶ Glue stick

Diff./Time

Easy

1 hour

Organize child socks in cylinders of corrugated paper lined with patterned paper and tied together with a ribbon.

1 Cut the Paper

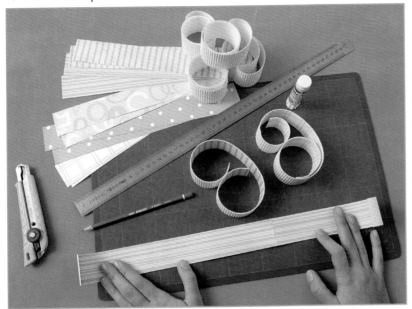

With a pencil, draw five 1 1/2x20 1/16 in. (4x30 cm) strips on the smooth side of the corrugated paper and two 1 1/2x11 3/4 in. (4x30 cm) strips on each sheet of scrapbooking paper. Cut them out.

IDEA. *Place the composition directly into a drawer lined with blue paper.*

IDEA. *Make a similar organizer for other types of underwear by altering the height and length of the strips.*

Glue the Strips

Smear the glue stick along the smooth side of a corrugated strip. Adhere a strip of scrapbooking paper on top, starting from one end and working towards the other. Smooth to eliminate the air bubbles. Glue on another strip of the same paper next to the first to cover the entire length of the corrugated strip. Cover all five corrugated paper strips with scrapbooking paper strips of different patterns.

2 Roll Up the Strips

Roll up the ends of every strip to form two cylinders about 2 in. (5 cm) in diameter. Secure each cylinder with a clothespin. Make a hole through two thicknesses of corrugated paper with a hatpin. Insert a paper fastener into each hole (if necessary enlarge the holes with the tip of the scissors). Spread the tabs to block the paper fastener in place.

3 Attach the Buttons

Choose a different paper fastener for each strip of corrugated paper. Arrange the five components to form a circle. Encircle with the white and blue checkered ribbon and tie a bow on the side. Using glue dots, center and attach buttons onto the corrugated paper as decoration. Insert a pair of socks into each cylinder.

Medals on Display

Tools

- Pencil
- Ruler
- Utility knife
- Cutting mat
- Bone folder
- Hole punch (5/32 in., 4 mm in diameter)
- Circle craft punch (1 in., 2.5 cm in diameter)
- Scissors
- Flat-tipped paintbrush
- Paper clamps

Materials

- 8x9 in. (20x23 cm) sheets of Finnboard, 1/16 in. (2 mm) thick
- Multi-colored striped scrapbooking paper
- Pink polka dot scrapbooking paper
- A4 brown paper
- Gold fleur-de-lis stickers
- Double-sided tape
- Double-sided adhesive foam pads
- Glue pen
- Elmer's glue

Diff./Time

Medium

3 hours

With your own hands, create original medals to display in a Finnboard frame covered in scrapbooking paper.

1 Make the Ribbons

Cut six 1x3 1/2 in. (2.8x9.2 cm) strips of striped scrapbooking paper (choose different colors for each strip). Following the diagram below, trace the folding reference lines (broken lines) with a pencil on the back of the stripes. Score the lines with a bone folder. Fold every strip in half and push the corners inwards to form two small "valley" folds.

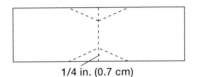

1/4 in. (0.7 cm)

2 Attach the Medals

Cut the medals out of the gold stickers: using a utility knife, cut out the fleur-de-lis or punch them out with the circle craft punch. You can use either the flowers themselves or their negatives. Make a hole at the top of the medals with the hole punch. Cut thin strips from the rest of gold stickers. Thread the strips through the holes in the medals and glue to the paper ribbons with the glue pen. Glue horizontal strips across the center of the ribbons and fold the ends over the edges.

Enlarge the diagram

by 200% in a photocopier

3 Make the Display Frame

Cut a 9x10 1/4 in. (23x26 cm) rectangle of pink polka dot scrapbooking paper and an 8x9 in. (20x23 cm) rectangle of brown paper. Coat one side of the Finnboard sheets with Elmer's glue and adhere the polka dot rectangle. Cut the corners of the paper at an angle. Coat the flaps with glue and fold over the edges. Glue a fleur-de-lis at the top of the display to serve as a hanger. Coat the uncovered side of the Finnboard with Elmer's glue and adhere the brown paper rectangle. From the other finnbpard sheet, cut a 5/8 in. (1.5 cm) wide frame.

4 Cut the Paper for Covering the Frame

From the pink polka dot paper, cut 4 strips: two 1 3/4x8 in. (4.3x20 cm) and two 1 3/4x9 in. (4.3x23 cm). Make 1/4 in. (5 mm) incisions along the long edges and 5/8 in. (1.5 cm) incisions along the short edges of the strips.

Cover the Frame

Coat one of the long sides of the Finnboard frame with Elmer's glue (front, back and edges). Center a strip and adhere well, folding over and pressing the 1/4 in. (5 mm) flaps over the edges for the entire length of the side. Using scissors, cut the external corners of the strip at 45°. Do the same thing on the other side. Secure with paper clips until the glue is completely dry. Repeat the procedure along the short sides matching the obliquely cut corners.

5 Assemble the Frame

Attach the frame to the backing with double-sided tape. Fold over the top 1/16 in. (2 mm) of the medal ribbons. Attach the double-sided adhesive foam pads to the medals and adhere to the display. Arrange the medals in two rows, alternating the colors of the ribbons.

Rocket Container

Tools

- Utility knife
- Cutting mat
- Ruler
- Pencil
- Scissors
- Flat-tipped paintbrush
- Clothespins

Materials

- Silver and green corrugated paper
- Multi-colored craft foam circles, 1 in. (2.5 cm) in diameter
- Small multi-color paper fasteners
- Elmer's glue
- Adhesive tape

Diff./Time

👁 👁 👁
Easy

⧗ ⧗ ⧗
30 min.

This fun rocket-shaped container will be particularly useful when giving a poster as a present.

1 Cut the Components

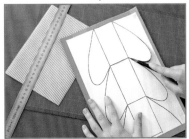

Attach a photocopy of the drawing below to the back of the corrugated green paper, with the ribbing oriented vertically, with adhesive tape. Cut out the three units that will form the tail of the rocket. On differently colored corrugated paper, trace a 6x8 in. (15x20 cm) rectangle with the long side parallel to the ribbing and cut it out.

TRICK. Stick pieces of adhesive tape over the tabs of the paper fasteners so that the poster does not get caught on them as you slide it into the cylinder.

Enlarge the diagram by 285%.

2 Decorate

Using a utility knife, make a small incision in the centers of the craft foam circles and of the three tail units. Also, make three similar incisions in the rectangle, 2 in. (5 cm) apart. Attach the circles to the rectangle with paper fasteners.

3 Glue the Tail Units

Coat the fins of the three tail units with Elmer's glue and glue them together fin to fin. Use clothespins to keep them together while they dry.

4 Assemble the Rocket

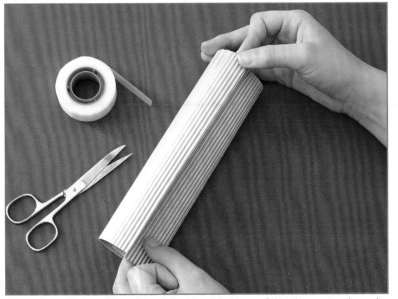

Close the cylinder with a strip of double-sided tape. Slide the poster through the cylinder and into the tail section.

Adjust the Body of the Rocket to Fit the Poster

Measure the poster's short side. Cut the body of the rocket from corrugated paper: the longer side of the rectangle should be the same size, or slightly longer or shorter than the poster's short side (the tail section of the rocket, on the other hand, does not need adjustment). Don't secure the poster with rubber bands before inserting it into the rocket.

Cat Piggy Bank

- Pencil
- Ruler
- Precision knife
- Cutting mat
- Scissors

Materials

- Foam board, 3/16 in. (5 mm) thick (two 1x1 3/8 in. [2.5x3.5 cm] pieces)
- White tissue paper (two A4 sheets)
- Décopatch paper, red with white polka dots (n. 422)
- White and orange checkered décopatch paper (n. 322)
- Cardboard cat
- Black permanent marker
- 8 in. (20 cm) of red satin ribbon
- Universal fast-drying adhesive
- Spray adhesive

Diff./Time

Easy

1 hour

This sweet kitty piggy bank covered in patterned paper will take good care of your little one's savings.

1 Cover the Cat

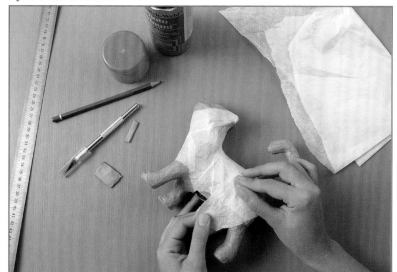

Along the back of the cat, draw and cut a 1/4x1 1/4 in. (0.7x3 cm) opening with a precision knife. On the belly, make a 1x1 1/4 in. opening and trim the edges. Coat the cat in white tissue paper.

2 Cut the Paper

From the red polka dot Décopatch paper, cut seventeen ovals of different sizes, two small white dots for the eyes, two small red triangles with rounded corners for the ears and one even more rounded triangle for the nose. From the white and orange checkered Décopatch paper, cut two or three triangles with very rounded corners.

Glue On the Tissue Paper

Tear several strips of white tissue paper. Coat one strip with spray adhesive and glue it to the cat (smooth well with your fingers making sure the paper follows the curves of the cardboard). Glue on the other strips in the same way, overlapping them slightly.

3 Glue On the Details

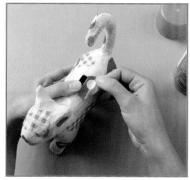

Using spray adhesive, attach each colored piece of paper to the cat (overlap the red ovals with pieces of white and orange checkered paper).

4 Finish the Details

Using a black marker, trace the edges of the eyes and make a black dot for each pupil. Tie the red ribbon around the neck.

5 Make the Plug

Glue the two small pieces of foam board together using fast-drying adhesive. Trace the edge of the piece of cardboard cut from the cat's belly onto the foam board. Cut out using a precision knife. Cover this "plug" with white tissue paper and use it to close the piggy bank.

SUGGESTION. *Set up a "gluing station" using a rather large cardboard box. Place the paper in need of gluing inside the box and spray with the spray adhesive. This way, glue particles will not diffuse throughout the room. If possible, work outdoors or in a well-aerated room.*

Eyeglass Case

Tools

▶ Pencil
▶ Ruler
▶ Utility knife
▶ Cutting mat
▶ Scissors
▶ Circle craft punch (1 1/8 in., 2.8 cm in diameter)
▶ Bone folder
▶ Compass

Materials

▶ Card stock A4 (250 g/m2)
▶ Orange patterned scrapbooking paper
▶ A5 pink paper
▶ A5 white paper
▶ A5 black paper
▶ Black marker
▶ Glue stick

Diff./Time

Medium

1 hour

Make your children happy by making them an eyeglass case that looks like a very sleepy cat!

1 Cut Out the Components

Photocopy the diagram to the right onto orange card stock. Cut along the solid lines with a utility knife. Score along the broken lines with a bone folder. Place the ear template onto orange patterned scrapbooking paper and trace the edges with a pencil. Cut the ear out with scissors and fold the flap as shown in the diagram. Using the craft punch, punch two circles from the white paper. Using the compass, draw two circles: one with a diameter of 3/4 in. (1.8 cm) on pink paper and one with a diameter of 1/2 in. (1.3 cm) on black paper. Cut out the circles with scissors.

Score the Fold Lines

Position a ruler along the broken lines and score the folds with the bone folder. Fold along all the lines, leaving the eyes intact.

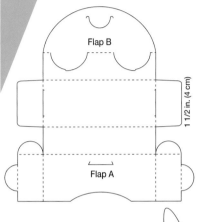

Flap B

1 1/2 in. (4 cm)

Flap A

Enlarge the diagram by 330% in a photocopier.

Ear

2 Create the Face (1)

Using a glue stick, glue the two white circles to the flat case. Cut the black circle in half. Glue the black semi-circles in the center of the white circles with the flat side facing up. Glue the flaps of each ear behind the eyes. Brush glue onto half of the pink circle. Glue the circle over the curved flap that will serve as the closure. Make two incisions to the sides of the pink circle.

3 Create the Face (2)

Using a black marker, outline the eyes and draw a line in correspondence the straight sides of the black semi-circles. Under the eyes, draw the cheeks with a pencil. Cut three 1/4x4 1/8 in. (0.5x10.5 cm) strips of black paper and insert them into one of the slits to the side of the nose and out the other. From the scrapbooking paper, cut two 1 3/4 in. long strips (you can vary the width). Glue the strips onto flap A, one next to the other. Trim the strips that extend beyond the edge with scissors. Cut a slit with the utility knife.

Glue the rectangle to flap B. Trim the paper so it is flush with flap B. Close the case by inserting the rounded edge into the slit in flap A.

4 Prepare the Rectangle

Cut a 1 3/4x4 5/16 in. (4.5x10.9 cm) rectangle of scrapbooking paper. Fold it lengthwise at 3/4 in. (2 cm) from the edge and position behind flap B (patterned side facing the flap, fold against fold). Trace the edges of the eyes on the outside of the case by lifting the two semi-circles and tracing the edges with a pencil. Cut along the lines with a utility knife. Position the rectangle fold against fold with the patterned side facing the flap and the rounded sides of the semi-circles towards the rounded edge of flap B once more. Fold the semi-circles back and insert them into the openings corresponding to the eyes in flap B.

IDEA. *Following the same procedure, you can also make a frog!*

5 Close the Case

Good Night, My Sweet!

Tools

- Pencil
- Eraser
- Ruler
- Utility knife
- Cutting mat
- Scissors
- Clocks stamp
- Alphabet stamps
- Manual riveter

Materials

- A4 sky-blue card stock
- A4 blue card stock
- A4 white card stock
- A4 tracing paper
- Blue ink pad
- Blue ballpoint pen
- Two small metal rivets (blue and gold)
- Blue Mouliné stranded cotton
- Glue stick

Diff./Time

Easy

30 min.

Every child will want to keep this sweet card with a lovable sheep wishing them good night in their room.

1 Cut the Card

Cut a 4x11 in. (10.5x28 cm) rectangle of sky blue card stock. Make a mark in the center of one of the long sides and fold the rectangle in half. Trace and cut out a 4 1/2x3 in. (11x7.5 cm) opening in one of the panels.

IDEA. If you don't have a stamp with clocks, replace it with a heart or number stamps.

2 Cut Out the Sheep

Using tracing paper, trace and transfer the drawing of the sheep onto white card stock. Cut it out with scissors.

TRICK. If you need to make many cards, photocopy the sheep with the text already printed on top.

Enlarge the template by 190% in a photocopier

3 Stamp the Card

Cut a 4x5 1/2 in. (10.5x14 cm) rectangle of blue card stock. Glue it to the card so it is visible through the opening. Using the clocks stamp and the blue ink pad, stamp clocks all over the surface of the blue rectangle. Draw the details of the sheep's head with a blue ballpoint pen.

4 Apply the Rivets

Using the manual riveter, make holes in the card stock and insert the blue rivet in the mark on the sheep and the gold rivet in the center of the top edge of the card's frame. Cut 1 1/2 in. (4 cm) of blue Mouliné cotton thread, pass it through the rivet in the frame and the sheep, and tie.

Compose the Text

Trace two parallel lines 3/4 in. (2 cm) from the top and 3/4 in. (2 cm) from the bottom on the sheep. Using the alphabet stamps and the blue ink pad, stamp the message on the two lines. Coat the stamps with ink before each application. After use, clean the stamps with soap and water.

Illuminating Teddy Bear

Tools

▶ Precision knife
▶ Cutting mat
▶ Scissors
▶ Black permanent marker

Materials

▶ 7x9 in. (18x23 cm) apple green glossy paper bag
▶ 6 3/4x6 3/4 in. (17x17 cm) sheet of semi-transparent turquoise paper
▶ 6 3/4x6 3/4 in. (17x17 cm) grey card stock
▶ 23 1/2 in. (60 cm) mauve silk taffeta ribbon, 1 1/2 in. (4 cm) wide
▶ Pocket light
▶ Removable adhesive tape
▶ Glue stick

Diff./Time

Easy

30 min.

With its soft and suffused light shining through a teddy bear-shaped cutout, this nightlight will help your child fall asleep.

1 Cut Out the Template

Place a photocopy of the drawing on the bottom of this page onto the card stock square. Cut out the teddy bear with a precision knife.

2 Trace the Drawing

Unthread the handles of the paper bag. Position the template on the bag, 2 in. (5 cm) from the bottom edge (so that the pocket light will not be visible). Secure the template with pieces of removable adhesive tape. Trace the edges of the teddy bear with the permanent marker. Detach the template.

3 Close the Paper Bag

Thread the taffeta ribbon through the holes in the bag. Tie it with a bow. Cut the ends of the ribbon at an angle. Turn on the pocket light. Crack open the bag, insert the light and position it with the light beam facing the teddy-bear opening straight on or at an angle, depending on the desired light intensity.

Cut the Paper Bag

Insert the card stock square into the bag. Using the precision knife, cut along the lines. Take out the card stock. On the interior of the bag, smear the edges of the teddy-bear opening with a glue stick. Adhere the square of transparent paper to the inside of the bag, making sure it sticks well.

TRICK. *To make sure there are no traces of the marker remaining on the nightlight, cut the paper bag just outside of the marker line.*

Enlarge the template by 200% in a photocopier.

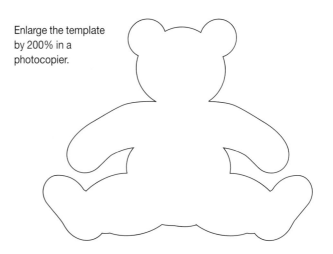

Kids' Parties

Card with a Cake

Tools

▶ Utility knife
▶ Ruler
▶ Cutting mat
▶ Bone folder

Materials

▶ A4 pale pink card stock
▶ A4 acid green card stock
▶ A4 white paper
▶ Yellow, pink and fuchsia markers
▶ Purple and gold glitter
▶ Glue stick
▶ Glue pen, clear

Diff./Time

Easy

30 min.

A birthday card hiding a two-tier cake with candles
and glitter is sure to be liked by little girls.

1 Make the Greeting Card

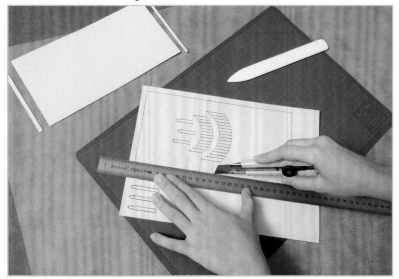

Transfer the diagrams on the bottom of this page onto pale pink card stock and cut along the border of the rectangle. Cut along all the solid lines (including the three candles). Cut a 10x5 in. (25x13 cm) rectangle of acid green paper.

Cut and Fold the Paper

Cut along all the solid lines using a ruler and a utility knife. Score along the broken lines with a bone folder (if you don't have this tool, you can use a large knitting needle with a round tip or an empty ballpoint pen); a utility knife may also work but you will have to be careful not to apply too much pressure on the blade so it doesn't cut through the paper.

2 Color the Candles

Insert a piece of paper under the card's candles and color with markers. Decorate the other four candles as well.

3 Give Volume

With your left hand, keep the card still. Place your right hand on the back of the card stock and gently push up on the thin strips of the cake tiers.

4 Decorate with Glitter

Glue the four candles onto the lower tier of the cake distributing them evenly. Apply some clear glue to the "flames" and sprinkle with gold glitter. Put some more glue on to the tops of the cake tiers and sprinkle with purple glitter.

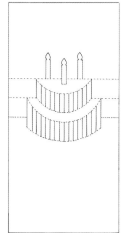

Enlarge the two diagrams by 400% in a photocopier.

5 Glue the Card Together

When the clear glue is completely dry, glue the pale pink card stock over the green and write your message.

Clown-Themed Party

Tools

▶ Pencil
▶ Eraser
▶ Ruler
▶ Precision knife
▶ Cutting mat
▶ Scissors
▶ Bone folder
▶ Compass

Materials

▶ 2x25 1/2 in. (8x65 cm) white fine-grained card stock (180 g/m2)
▶ A4 tracing paper A4
▶ A4 orange paper
▶ A4 red paper
▶ Scraps of patterned scrapbooking paper
▶ Black medium point marker
▶ Twelve round holographic stickers, 1/2 in. (13 mm) in diameter
▶ Twelve black round stickers, 1/4 in. (8 mm) in diameter
▶ Six white round stickers, 1/4 in. (8 mm) in diameter
▶ Black alphabet stickers
▶ Glue stick

Diff./Time

Easy

1 hour

Nothing is better than this accordion fold card with fun clowns on every page for inviting your friends to a playful party.

1 Fold the Card

Divide the card stock strip into six parts by drawing a pencil line parallel to the short side every 4 1/4 in. (10.8 cm) with a pencil. Using a bone folder, score folds along the pencil lines. Erase the marks. Fold like an accordion and round off the four corners.

2 Cut the Components

Using tracing paper, copy and trace the hair twelve times onto the orange paper and the hats twelve times onto the scrapbooking paper scraps. Draw twelve 1 1/2 in. circles on the red paper with the compass. Cut out all the components with scissors.

Enlarge the template by 300% in a photocopier.

TRICK. *You can cut out the red noses with a circle drawing stencil and a rotary cutter.*

3 Assemble the Faces

Assemble the clown faces. Glue a red circle onto every page of the card, overlapping the border and centering along the width. Glue on the hair shapes extending them beyond the upper border by about 1/2 in. (15 mm). Glue on the hats at angles.

Align the Components Well

To align the parts of the clown face on the fronts and backs of the different pages perfectly, fold the pages as you go and position the noses, hair and hats in perfect correspondence with those already glued down. If the components are not perfectly flush, trim them with scissors.

IDEA. *Only the hair, hats and noses are glued to the front and back. Ask your children to finish the clown faces on the back of the card with other stickers.*

4 Draw the Details

Stick two holographic stickers above the clowns' noses. Position two black stickers along the edges of the holographic stickers: depending on the position of the black sticker, the clown will appear to peek out, look to the side, look up etc. Draw eyebrows of different shapes with a black marker. Finally, stick on a white sticker onto the side of the nose.

5 Compose the Text

Compose the text with the alphabet stickers: detach the letters from their backing with the tip of a utility knife and adhere them to the page of the card (angle each word differently).

Birthday Party

Tools

- Pencil
- Ruler
- Cutting mat
- Precision knife
- Scissors
- Utility knife
- Compass
- Bone folder
- Two brushes for stenciling (stencil and round brush)
- Cups
- Cotton swabs

Materials

- Tablecloth of non-woven fabric
- White card stock
- Colored paper
- Paper cups of different colors
- Tracing paper
- Colored strings
- Colored chenille wire
- Assorted acrylic paints
- Colored acrylic paint markers
- Repositionable spray adhesive
- Glue stick

Diff./Time

Medium

2 hours

Explanation on 2 spreads

Brighten up a children's birthday party by making cheerful garlands and decorating the tablecloth and cups with lively balloons.

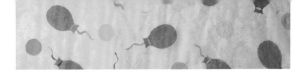

THE TABLECLOTH

1 Make the Stencil

Copy the drawing of the smaller balloon onto a piece of tracing paper and carefully cut it out with a precision knife. Using a compass, draw a 1 1/2 in. (4 cm) circle on a sheet of tracing paper. Cut it out with a precision knife. Make a stencil for each color that you plan on using.

2 Paint the Balloons

Using repositionable spray adhesive glue a balloon stencil to the tablecloth. Transfer a small amount of acrylic paint onto white card stock. Load a stencil brush with paint, remove the excess and paint all the balloons of the same color, tilting the stencil differently for every balloon.

Paint Using Stencils

Glue the stencil to the surface to be painted to ensure it does not shift. Dab with a paint-loaded brush in the opening of the stencil then allow to dry. Delicately detach the stencil and move it to another location on the tablecloth. Paint all the balloons of the same color. Change stencils and colors. Between colors, wash the brush in a glass full of water and dry well.

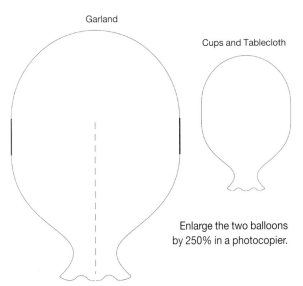

Garland

Cups and Tablecloth

Enlarge the two balloons by 250% in a photocopier.

3 Paint the Circles

Paint the circles between the balloons using the stencil prepared earlier.

4 Paint the Balloon Strings

Using the round brush, paint the balloon strings. Allow to dry.

THE GARLAND

1 Fold Like an Accordion

Cut four 6 3/4x13 in. (17x33 cm) strips of colored paper. Using a bone folder, score a fold every 4 5/16 in. (11 cm) and fold like an accordion. Glue the strips together end to end alternating colors.

2 Transfer the Balloon Drawing

Trace the larger balloon onto white card stock. Cut along the lines. Place the template onto the top panel of the long strip folded like an accordion (the thicker lines should be flush with the edges of the paper) and trace it.

3 Cut Out the Balloons

Using a utility knife, trim the paper along the lines without cutting the sides. Unfold the strip obtaining a garland of colorful balloons 47 1/4 in. (120 cm) long.

4 Decorate the Balloons

Draw colored dots with the round brush dipped in acrylic paints. Cut 11 3/4 in. (30 cm) strings and tie them around the bottoms of the balloons. Make holes in the two ends of the garland with the tip of the compass. Pass a string through each hole so you can hang the garland.

THE CUPS

IDEA. After the party, every child could take a cup decorated with a balloon with their name on it home.

1 Cut Out the Balloons

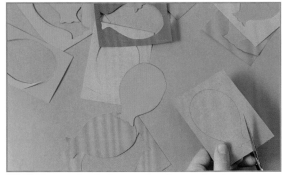

Trace the smaller balloon onto pieces of colored paper. Cut the balloons along the lines (count one balloon for each child).

2 Write the Names

Using acrylic paint markers, write the names of the children in the center of each balloon (use different colors to create contrast).

3 Decorate the Balloons

Decorate with dots using cotton swabs dipped directly into tubs of acrylic paint.

4 Attach the Balloons to the Cups

Make two parallel 3/8 in. (1 cm) long incisions, 3/8 in. (1 cm) from the edge of the cups (not any lower or it will be impossible to fill it). Cut the chenille wire into pieces about 8 in. (20 cm) long. Wrap them around the bottoms of the balloons and pass the ends through the slits in the cups. Loop the ends of the wire so that the children don't hurt themselves.

Airplane Napkin Holders

Tools	Materials	Diff./Time
▶ Pencil ▶ Ruler ▶ Utility knife ▶ Cutting mat ▶ Scissors ▶ Rotary cutter ▶ Compass with adaptor	FOR ONE AIRPLANE: ▶ 11 3/4 in. (30 cm) square of double-sided patterned scrapbooking paper ▶ Large triangular, rectangular and circular stickers of different colors ▶ Black alphabet stickers (between 1 1/4 and 1 3/4 in. [30 - 45 mm] tall) ▶ Colored paper fastener ▶ Universal fast-drying adhesive	 Easy 2 hours

For an unforgettable snack, make colorful airplane-shaped napkin holders personalized with the names of the little pilots.

1 Cut the Paper

Photocopy and cut out the image on the right. Place it onto a sheet of scrapbooking paper and trace. Cut along solid lines with a utility knife. Attach the rotary cutter to the compass and set the radius to 1 1/2 in. (3.7 cm) for the wing tips and to 3/4 in. (2 cm) for the small quarter-circles and for the rudder. Cut one 1 1/2x4 1/4 in. (4x11 cm) and one 2x3/4 in. (5x1 cm) rectangles.

2 Assemble the Wings

With the more brightly colored of the scrapbooking paper sides on the outside, slide the two slits in the wing piece into each other. Fold the airplane rudder following the broken lines. Apply glue to the semi-circle of the rudder and glue together folding along the central line. Insert the rudder into the slit in the wings. Fold over and glue its two flaps under the wings.

Enlarge the templates by 285% in a photocopier.

3 Assemble the Cockpit

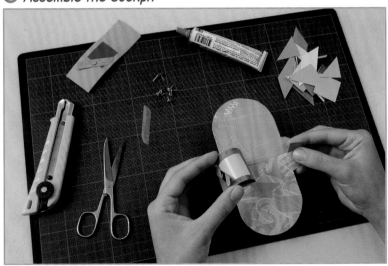

Fold the 1 1/2x4 1/4 in. (4x11 cm) rectangle (cockpit) 1 1/4 in. (3 cm) from the short edges. On the side of the paper opposite to the one used for the wings, attach a rectangular sticker of contrasting color. Make a small cross with the utility knife, 1/8 in. (4 mm) from one of the folds. Attach the paper fastener (the propeller) to the cockpit. Glue the paper flaps one on top of the other. Glue the cockpit on top of the wings in front of the rudder.

4 Decorate the Airplanes

Place one large triangular sticker over the airplane wing junction (attach triangles of different colors cut from patterned paper with a more subdued design along the airplane wings). Compose the names with alphabet stickers alternating capital with lower case letters. Adhere a round sticker to the airplane rudder.

SUGGESTION. *Insert brightly colored napkins into these holders!*

Make the Propeller

Make a small cross with the utility knife in the center of the 3/4 in. (1 cm) wide strip cut in step 1. Round off one corner at each end of the strip-propeller with scissors, one along the top and the other along the bottom edge.

Lollypops on Show

Tools

▶ Pencil
▶ Ruler
▶ Utility knife
▶ Cutting mat
▶ Scissors
▶ Punch
▶ Hand-held hole punch
  (1/8 in. [3 mm] in diameter)
▶ Flat-tipped paintbrush

Materials

▶ Styrofoam ball, 4 in. (10 cm) in diameter
▶ Pink Decopatch paper n. 292
▶ Patterned scrapbooking paper
▶ Thirteen lollypops
▶ Thirteen gold rivets
▶ Organza ribbons, about 1/2 in. (1 cm) wide
▶ Adhesive tape
▶ Decopatch all-in-one glue and sealer
▶ Universal fast-drying adhesive

Diff./Time

Medium

45 min.

Brighten-up snack time for your children with this display
of lollypops decorated with ribbons.

1 Prepare the Base

Cut twenty 7 3/4x1/2 in. (19x1 cm) strips of pink Décopatch paper. Using the utility knife, cut the Styrofoam sphere in half.

2 Glue the Paper

Apply the Decopatch glue and sealer to one of the semi-spheres and adhere the first strip of paper (for each strip, apply starting from the bottom edge, lay over the top and then fold under the opposite edge). Apply another coat of Decopatch glue and sealer over the strip being careful to remove any excess. Repeat the process with the other strips until the entire semi-sphere is covered.

Cut the Styrofoam

Insert a new blade into the utility knife. Extract 1 1/4 in. (3 cm) of the blade length and block it. Take hold of the sphere with your left hand and place the blade onto the centerline with your right hand. Follow this line around the sphere inserting the blade to a depth of 1/2 in. (1 cm). When you have gone all the way around, repeat inserting the blade deeper until you have two semi-spheres.

TRICK. If you don't have a punch, you can use a knitting needle.

3 Insert the Rivets

Using the punch, make one hole in the top of the semi-sphere. Then, make four holes around and 5/8 in. (1.5 cm) away from the first, four more 1 1/4 in. (3 cm) away, and last four holes 1 3/4 in. (4.5 cm) away from the center. Widen each hole with the punch and insert the rivets securing them with a dot of fast-drying adhesive.

4 Decorate

Cut twelve strips of scrapbooking paper, about 6 in. (15 cm) long and 5/8 in. (1.5 cm) wide. Join the ends of each strip with adhesive tape to form rings. Flatten the rings with your fingers and punch a hole through two thicknesses of paper where they join. Thread two flattened rings onto each of six lollypop sticks. Tie a piece of ribbon around the other lollypops. Insert the lollypops into the base.

SUGGESTION. The lollypop wrappers were removed for a better visual effect. You can wrap them with squares of plastic wrap while they wait to be sampled!

A "Dress" for the Cake

Tools

▶ Pencil
▶ Ruler
▶ Utility knife
▶ Cutting mat
▶ Scissors
▶ Compass with extension bar
▶ Medium hole punch

Materials

▶ A4 white card stock
▶ 20x25 1/2 in. (50x65 cm) gold card stock (250 g/m2)

Diff./Time

Easy

30 min.

Celebrate your child's birthday in an original way by surrounding the candle-bearing birthday cake with a golden "dress."

1 Cut Out the Template

Transfer the diagram to the right onto white card stock and cut along the lines with scissors or a utility knife. This wrap will fit around a cake with a diameter of 8 in. (20 cm): you can modify the size of the template and the circles described in step 2 to fit your baking pan.

3 Cut the Shape

Using a utility knife and a ruler, cut the lines perpendicular the two circles. Cut the external edge with scissors or a utility knife.

Cut with Precision

Use a utility knife to cut along the smooth curved lines and the straight lines (in the latter case, use a ruler to guide the blade) so that the resulting cuts are clean and precise. For the irregular curved lines, use decoupage scissors or a precision knife.

2 Trace the Shape

On the back of the gold card stock, make a mark in the center. Position the tip of the compass on top and draw two circles: one with a diameter of 7 1/4 in. (18.5 cm) and one with a diameter of 15 3/4 in. (40 cm). Position the template between the two circles so that the upper and lower edges of the template are flush with the circles. Using a pencil, trace the template, including the triangle and the slit. Shift and trace the template along the entire area delimited by the circles.

IDEA. *You can also use this covering to decorate a salad bowl or a vase!*

Enlarge the diagram to 400% in a photocopier.

4 Fold the Paper

Place the cake pan in the center of the form. Fold the "petals" against the external side of the pan one at a time, inserting the sharp-pointed tabs into the slits on the left side of the "petals." Fold the overlapping vignette elements outwards. Using a hole punch, make holes in the vignettes above the triangles.

Surprise Crackers

Tools

▶ Pencil
▶ Ruler
▶ Utility knife
▶ Cutting mat
▶ Scissors
▶ Decorative-edge scissors
▶ Circle craft punch (1 1/4 in., 3 cm) in diameter
▶ Needle

Materials

FOR ONE CRACKER, 10 1/4 IN. (26 CM) LONG:

▶ 5 3/4x7 1/4 in. (14.5 x18.5 cm) multi-colored checkered scrapbooking paper
▶ 5 3/4x7 1/4 in. (14.5 x18.5 cm) white paper (120 g/m2)
▶ 4 3/4x7 1/4 in. (12x18.5 cm) green tissue paper
▶ 1 1/2x4 in. (4x10 cm) red paper ▶ White and red ink pads
▶ Two 8x14 1/4 in. (20x36 cm) strips of white non-woven fabric
▶ Eight paper mache balls ▶ Colored rub-on letteres
▶ 11 3/4 in. (30 cm) of white plastic-coated wire, 1/16 in. (2 mm) thick
▶ Eight double-sided adhesive foam squares
▶ Removable adhesive tape
▶ Spray adhesive ▶ Universal fast-drying adhesive

Diff./Time

Medium

30 min.

Great for both older and younger kids, these cute paper candies hide a mysterious surprise inside.

1 Glue the Paper

Using spray adhesive, glue the checkered paper to the white paper. On the white paper, draw a line parallel to the long sides and centered along the width with a pencil. Using decorative-edge scissors, cut the paper along the line. Reunite the two pieces of paper and secure together with pieces of reusable adhesive tape. Using spray adhesive, glue the green tissue paper to the back. Remove the adhesive tape.

Make a Brea-Apart Object

The delicate tissue paper glued to the inside of the cracker keeps the two halves of the candy together while allowing it to open simply when the ends are pulled! Using the same technique, you can make any type of break-apart packet. To make it easier to open the paper object, position a string along the inside, between two strips of adhesive tape. Pass the string to the outside: take hold of the end of the string and pull it, neatly cutting through the paper along the taped line.

2 Attach the Frilling

Fold the non-woven fabric to obtain a 4 1/4x14 1/4 in. (11x36 cm) strip. Pour a line of fast-drying adhesive along one of the long sides of the rectangle, on the side of the green tissue paper. Glue the non-woven fabric frill facing outwards, folding it onto itself to form half an inch (1 cm) pleats. Repeat along the other side.

3 Compose the Text

Using the rub-on letters, compose the words of your choice on the squares of a rectangle of scrapbooking paper. Cut the small squares out with scissors. Attach a double-sided adhesive foam pad under each square. Attach the squares to the rectangle, four on each side of the central cut made with the decorative-edge scissors. Stain the edges of the scrapbooking paper with the red ink pad.

4 Form the Cracker

Form the cylinder: pour a line of glue along one of the two sides of the rectangle with the frills, and close the cylinder. Punch four circles out of the red paper. Using the white ink pad, stain the edges of the red circles with white ink. Cut the plastic-coated wire in half. Twist the ends around a pencil leaving 1 or 1 1/2 in. (3 or 4 cm) of the tips straight. Pierce the paper mache balls with the needle. String a ball, a red circle and another ball onto the straight length at the end of each wire. Secure everything with a dot of glue to the wire tip. Gather the frilling and tie with the decorated wire, after having hidden a surprise inside.

TRICK. *If you don't have double-sided foam squares, cut a small slice from a cork and stick pieces of double-sided tape on its faces.*

53

Frog

Tools	Materials	Diff./Time
▶ Pencil ▶ Ruler ▶ Utility knife ▶ Cutting mat ▶ Scissors ▶ Riveting kit (hammer and punch)	▶ 16x23 1/2 in. (40x60 cm) white card stock (300 g/m2) ▶ A5 paper: white, red and pale pink (125 g/m2) ▶ Tracing paper ▶ Four round black stickers ▶ Two paper fasteners ▶ 31 1/2 in. (80 cm) of patterned ribbon ▶ Green spray paint ▶ Double-sided tape ▶ Glue stick	 **Easy** **1 hour**

Seize the chance offered by Halloween or a children's party to make this funny frog-shaped mask!

1 Cut Out the Components

Using tracing paper, copy and transfer the drawings of the legs and head onto white card stock. Trace template A onto white paper two times, template B onto pale pink paper and template C onto red paper. Cut out all the components. Using the punch and the hammer, make holes where indicated.

2 Paint the Frog

Spray on several coats of green paint onto the card stock head and legs.

Enlarge the templates of the legs by 580% in a photocopier.

3 Glue the Mouth and Eyes

Smear the back of the pink component with the glue stick and adhere on top of the red semi-circle. Using pieces of double-sided tape, attach the mouth and the eyes to the head of the frog. Place a round black sticker on each eye and under each nostril.

IDEA. *You can substitute the round black stickers with two wiggle eyes.*

Paint with Spray Paint

When using spray paint, place the component that needs painting inside a large cardboard box to protect against paint spatter. Air the room where you work well. If this is not possible, work outdoors. Hold the can at a distance of about 8 in. (20 cm) from the surface being painted and apply many thin coats, allowing the paint to dry between each coat. Spray paint has a very strong odor: prepare the mask at least 24 hours before use.

4 Attach the Legs

To give the mask shape, close the gaps in the sides by overlapping the pairs of holes located by the straight sides. Insert paper fasteners into the holes and spread the tabs on the back.

5 Attach the Ribbons

Cut two 16 in. (40 cm) long pieces of ribbon. Tie a double knot at one end of each ribbon and thread the other ends through the mask's remaining holes.

Enlarge the templates of the head by 580% in a photocopier.

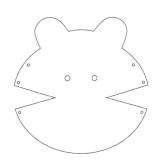

Flower Hats

Tools

- Pencil
- Ruler
- Utility knife
- Cutting mat
- Scissors
- Compass with extension
- Riveting kit (hammer and punch 9/32 in. [7 mm] in diameter)

Materials

FOR ONE HAT:
- Double-sided red/pink scrapbooking paper
- Green stripe-felt-marked paper, 8 in. (20 cm) square
- Tracing paper
- Tissue paper sheets of various colors
- Turquoise ink pad
- Green gift-wrapping ribbon
- Double-sided tape
- Rubber cement

Diff./Time

Easy

30 min.

Children will enjoy pretending to be elves and coming up with fantastical stories while wearing these hats.

1 Cut Out the Hat

Using a compass, draw a circle with a radius of 8 1/4 in. (21 cm) on some red scrapbooking paper. Inside, draw another circle with a radius of 6 1/4 in. (16 cm). Set the compass to a radius of 2 in. (5 cm). Positioning the needle along the inner circle, draw seven semicircles in a row. Using the template below, cut out the part of the circle (equal to two petals) that will allow to form a cone. Cut around the seven petals with scissors. Score the folds by lightly tracing them with a utility knife. Make a hole in the center of the hat.

TRICK. *To keep the hats from falling off the head, glue two rather long pieces of gift-wrapping ribbon to the inside of the hat, close to the edges of two opposite petals, and tie them under the chin.*

2 Make the Leaf

Using tracing paper, copy and transfer the shape of a leaf of your choosing onto green paper. Cut out with scissors. Cut a 2 1/4x3 in. (6x8 cm) rectangle from scraps of green paper. Brush some rubber cement onto one side of the rectangle. Roll it up tightly to form a stem with a diameter of 1/4 in. (6 mm). Hold tightly until dry.

3 Decorate the Hat

Cut circles with a diameter of 1 1/4 in. (3 cm) from sheets of tissue paper. Glue to the hat with rubber cement, overlapping some. Fold the leaf in half. Using the turquoise ink pad, stain the edges and the central vein of the leaf and one end of the stem.

4 Assemble the Components

Cut a 6 1/4 in. (16 cm) length of double-sided tape and position it along the side of the hat that is flush with the last petal (on the inside). Place a piece of double-sided tape of the same length on the side without the petal (on the outside). Overlap the two sides forming a cone. Press down hard to make sure they adhere well. Lift the petals. Cut a 23 1/2 in. (60 cm) length of gift-wrapping ribbon and curl it with the blade of the scissors. Thread 1 1/4 in. (3 cm) of its length through the hole in the top of the hat and glue it to the interior. Attach the leaf with its base facing the top of the hat using a piece of double-sided tape along the hat's seam.

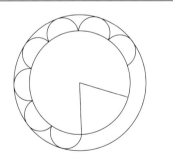

Enlarge the templates
by 1450% in a photocopier.

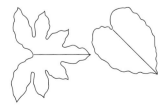

Attach the Stem

Using scissors, cut two 1 1/4 in. slits in the end of the stem not stained with ink. Lift the resulting paper flaps and brush with rubber cement. Insert the stem into the hat pushing the ink stained end out of the top. Press the stem flaps to the underside of the hat and hold down for a few moments.

Butterfly Fairy

Tools
- Pencil ▸ Eraser
- Ruler ▸ Scissors
- Utility knife ▸ Needle
- Cutting mat
- Bone folder
- Stapler
- Cotton swabs
- 20 in. (50 cm) of twine
- Cardboard 1 1/2x3 in. (4x8 cm)

Materials
- 20x25 1/2 (50x65 cm) card stock (160 g/m2)
- 20x25 1/2 in. (50x65 cm) blue polka dot paper
- 20x27 1/2 in. (50x70 cm) natural white paper
- Natural paper: pastel yellow, light blue and pink
- 6x20 in. (15x50 cm) silver paper
- 12 1/2 in. (32 cm) wood rod with a diameter of 3/8 in. (1 cm)
- White sewing thread
- Multi-color butterfly spangles
- Two small pink pompons
- Spray adhesive
- Universal fast-drying adhesive
- Rubber cement

Diff./Time

Medium

1 hour and 30 min.

Prepare a magic wand and a fairy hat decorated with colorful butterflies for your little girl and make her dreams come true!

1 Make the Cone

Adhere the polka dot paper onto card stock with spray adhesive. Cut a 3x20 in. (8x50 cm) strip of the polka dot paper and glue it around the wood rod using rubber cement. Draw a quarter of a circle with a radius of 20 in. (50 cm) on the card stock. Cut along the right angle, leaving a 3/4-1 1/4 in. (2-3 cm) margin along one of the edges, and then cut along the arc. Brush rubber cement onto the flap. Unite the straight edges to form a cone and press down.

Draw the Large Circles

Tie the twine to the tip of a pencil to transform it into a sort of large compass. Hold down the other end of the twine with one hand and trace a quarter of a circle with the other.

4 Cut Out the Butterflies

Cut out the template and position it on the back of silver paper. Trace it and cut it out (for the hat). Fold the rest of the paper in two and glue it back to back with spray adhesive. Place the butterfly template onto the silver paper ones more, trace it and cut it out (for the wand).

2 Fold the Paper

Cut two 2 3/4x27 1/2 in. (7x70 cm) pink, two 2x27 1/2 in. (5x70 cm) yellow, two 1 1/4x27 1/2 in. (3.5x70 cm) light blue and two 3/4x27 1/2 in. (2x70 cm) white strips of natural paper. Glue strips of the same color end to end forming four 55 in. (140 cm) strips. Using the 1 1/2x3 in. (4x8 cm) cardboard make equal folds along the entire length of the pink strip securing with dollops of rubber cement. Repeat for the other strips. Make the frill by sewing the four strips together with large straight stitches of white thread. For the veil, cut a quarter of a circle with a radius of 14 1/4 in. (36 cm) of white paper and accordion fold. Glue the top inch or so (a few centimeters) to secure the folding. For the wand, cut quarter circles from the four different color papers with radii of 11, 10 1/4, 9 1/2, and 8 3/4 in. (28, 26, 24 and 22 cm). Accordion fold. Stack them and glue the tips to form a fan.

5 Glue On the Butterflies

Attach a butterfly spangle over each staple with fast-drying adhesive. Apply more butterflies between the ones already glued down. Glue the silver butterfly to the hat. Glue a small pompon to the head of the butterfly. Glue some butterfly spangles onto the hat and onto the silver butterfly. Glue three butterflies together wing to wing around a cotton swab a small fraction of an inch (a few millimeters) from the cotton tip. Apply a dot of glue to the cotton tip and insert it into the top of the hat. Cut the cotton swab flush with the butterflies.

3 Attach the Veil and Frill

Glue the tip of the veil to the point of the cone and one of its sides along the seam with rubber cement. Position the frilling along the base of the cone so it extends beyond the edge and staple every 2 in. (5 cm). Glue one of the sides of the multi-colored fan down the length of the wand. Place a dab of rubber cement on the top of the wand and attach the tip of the fan. Trim away excess paper.

IDEA. *Complete the decoration with adhesive rhinestones.*

Enlarge the template by 285 % in a photocopier.

6 Finish the Wand

Glue the silver butterfly to the top of the wand and the pompon to the head of the butterfly. Glue five butterfly spangles along the length of the wand and two on the wings of the silver butterfly.

Royal Crown

Tools

- Pencil
- Ruler
- Utility knife
- Cutting mat
- Scissors
- Decorative-edge scissors
- Hatpin

Materials

- Havanna brown corrugated paper
- Gold spray paint
- Two large and seven small gold paper fasteners
- Seven pins with light blue heads
- Seven gold beads
- Seven gold paper stars
- Flower-shaped blue rhinestones (three big, four medium and seven small)
- 21 3/4 in. (55 cm) of light blue satin ribbon
- Glue dots
- Double-sided tape
- Glue stick

Diff./Time

Easy

45 min.

Great for a costume party, this crown decorated with a ribbon and flowers will give children a regal appearance.

1 Cut the Paper

On the smooth side of the paper, draw two strips: one 3 1/4x20 7/8 in. (8.5x53 cm) and one 1 3/4x20 7/8 in. (4.5x53 cm) in size. On the first strip, draw seven points using the drawing on this page as a guide. Using decorative-edge scissors cut along one of the sides of the second strip. Place the two strips onto old newspapers and spray with gold spray paint. Allow to dry. Turn the strips over and paint the back as well. Allow to dry once more.

2 Close the Crown

Attach a strip of double-sided tape onto one side of the satin ribbon. Center the satin ribbon on top of the strip with the decorative edge and adhere. Position this strip on top of the strip with the points. Overlap the two ends of the strips and make two holes with the hatpin. Close the crown using the two large paper fasteners. Punch holes in the crown bellow the ribbon and in line with each point. Insert small paper fasteners to hold the two layers of paper together.

3 Attach the Rhinestones

Place a dot of glue on the back of the flower rhinestones and attach them to the seven points of the crown alternating between the big and the medium flowers. In the same way, attach the small rhinestones to the light blue ribbon, below the valleys between the points.

IDEA. If you want to increase the diameter of the crown, draw one or two more points on the corrugated paper.

4 Glue On the Stars

Glue the paper stars onto the light blue satin ribbon between the rhinestones. Thread a gold bead onto each pin. Push the pins into the tips of crown's points.

Secure the Pins

If the paper ribbing is too large with respect to the diameter of the pins, dip the bodies of the latter into fast-drying adhesive and push into the corrugated paper. You can also wrap small pieces of removable adhesive squares around the bodies of the pins for the same purpose.

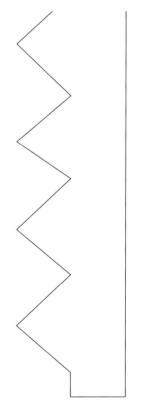

Enlarge the drawing by 300% in a photocopier.

Indian Headdress

Tools

- Pencil
- Precision knife
- Cutting mat
- Scissors
- Wave-edge scissors
- Glasses (1 1/2 and 2 1/4 in., 4 and 6 cm, in diameter)
- Needle

Materials

- Corrugated paper: red, orange, golden yellow, lemon yellow, blue and green
- Thick string of light blue wool or cotton
- Rubber band
- Wood beads of different colors
- Universal fast-drying adhesive

Diff./Time

Medium

1 hour and 30 min.

Make your little ones happy by making a headdress of a great Indian chief with multi-colored feathers just for them.

1 Cut the Components

Using the knife, cut one red feather A, two orange feathers B, two golden yellow feathers C, two lemon yellow feathers D, one blue feather D, two green feathers E, two lemon yellow feathers F, two blue feathers G, and two green feathers H (vertical ribbing). Cut the blue strip with wave-edge scissors.

2 Glue on the First Row

Glue the base of the largest feather to the center of the blue strip. Glue on the other feathers in order of decreasing size: start from the center and overlap the feathers inclining them slightly outwards as well.

3 Glue on the Second Row

Proceed in the same way for the second row of feathers, gluing the blue central feather first.

4 Assemble the Headdress

Cut out the red strip (vertical ribbing) with decorative-edge scissors and position it on top of the second row of feathers, covering their bases. Cut a 2 1/4 in. (6 cm) golden yellow circle and position it on top of the left end of the red strip, flush with the end of the blue strip. Cross stitch the circle and the strips together.

Sew the Components

Mark the needle entry points on the golden yellow circle and the red strip with a pencil (in the corners of 3/8 in. [1 cm] squares; leave 3/4 in. [2 cm] between each square). Pierce the marks with a needle or a punch. Using a thick thread, cross stitch the golden yellow circle to the red strip. Continue stitching together the red strip to the blue strip.

5 Make the Side Drops

Cut a circle with a diameter of 1 1/2 in. (4 cm) and mark the four holes for the stitching. Cut out one green feather I and one blue feather J. String the beads and the feathers onto a thick

TRICK. Sew a rubber band to the end of the red strip. In this way, the headdress will fit different size heads.

thread, and pass the thread back through the beads. Pass the two ends of the thread through the lower holes of the red circle from the back. Cross them on the front and pass them back through the upper holes. Position the red circle on top of the yellow and pass the two ends of the thread through the entire thickness of the headdress (yellow circle, blue and red stripes). Tie a knot on the back to secure the side drop. Cut out another two circles and two feathers, and repeat on the other side.

Enlarge by 485% in a photocopier. ➤

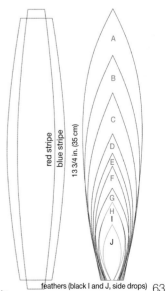

red stripe
blue stripe
13 3/4 in. (35 cm)

A
B
C
D
E
F
G
H
I
J

feathers (black I and J, side drops)

For the English edition:

WHITE STAR PUBLISHERS

WS White Star Publishers® is a registered trademark
belonging to De Agostini Libri S.p.A.

Translation and Editing: TperTradurre S.R.L.

© 2015 De Agostini Libri S.p.A.
Via G. da Verrazano, 15
28100 Novara, Italy
www.whitestar.it - www.deagostini.it

ISBN 978-88-544-0960-6
1 2 3 4 5 6   19 18 17 16 15

Printed in China